Try
2 See It
Through *My Eyes*

Written by Pratt the Poet

Elshamar Desktop Publishing

ISBN 13: 978-0-9748006-8-4

Table of Contents

Section One

The Game

"Game Over"

She blew my mind as she has done to the many men who have chosen her.

This goddess made love to my mind and kept me blind not knowing the game was already over.

I gave her the best years of my life and she only gave me heartache in return.

Worrying about if I would have to die for her love was the lesson I had to learn.

This game that I now hate once filled my pockets with plenty of paper.

And the way she blinded me gave me laughter at first and so many tears came later.

She still sleeps around with many men and most of them are too young to see.

When she began her manipulation of their minds the same as she did to me.

This woman has a constant hunger that can only be fed by money and lies.

You soon find yourself either in prison or dead and with either choice your soul surely dies.

This wicked woman which I speak of goes by her alias name of the "game".

She has destroyed and taken so many lives, she is a professional at causing pain.

So many of us have fallen for her beauty and felt that we could control her.

She has forced me to face reality, as I sit in the pen, and I realize that the game is over.

"Gotta Eat"

There are so many hungry souls who are forced to chase their next meal. They fully realize that they're in a chase because that meal won't standstill.

As a man, if your income won't let you wear the pants at home, that woman can become a nag.'

And if you can't find a legal way to eat, you may feel forced to pick up that bag.

Life is not always fair for people of color and those who are labeled as minorities.

It's a shame when you watch the evening news, and our shortcomings tend to be the top stories.

For many of us, we have young children that we must find a way to feed.

Sometimes our desperation forces poor decisions that only amplify our many needs.

We all get hungry and we can't always have a choice in our variety of food.

Our plans have been predestined to fail, and we wonder why we always lose.

Drugs, guns, and murder can place you in front of that judge's seat.

When we're forced to make another bad decision, now this penitentiary food is what you "gotta" eat.

"Ball Til You Fall"

Don't act as though you've never heard this street phrase. When you were getting that money, it was your hustler's code.

Few were blessed to leave this game and its crazy twisted maze, But for so many more this game was sold and not told.

When I say the game was sold, only you can negotiate this price. You either learn how to do this time or learn how to give up your life.

If you think that you're ballin', you're being investigated by the Feds. Yeah, PAC showed us all how, but now even our teacher is dead.

Watch your comrades closely, these days they carry knives and wear wires. The knife is for your back and those wires spark Federal fires.

It's your life, but don't be stupid though, only you can make the call Death patiently waits for you when you try to ball til' you fall.

"Mr. Pratt vs. Mr. D.P. (Only We Know)"

Hello, Mr. Pratt and how are you today? I pray that you are doing well my friend.

Mr. D.P., I'm not doing well at all, and I wonder daily when will the foolishness end?

End? Is that what's troubling us, don't waste another second on it, dog, we're gonna be cool.

Nah, you may be cool, but I awake daily heated and stress is what I'm going through.

But we woke up, count that blessing and realize that this time will serve to make us a better man.

That's what I keep hearing, but this part never seemed to be implemented into our master plan. Well, I think we did, let's see there's guns, dope, robbery and there's so much more, should I continue for you?

No! I've heard enough, you've proved your point, but don't forget if I was there, then you were too!

You are damn right I was there, so we know that this situation could have been a thousand times worse.

Maybe you're right, plus I can't argue with myself when you know each line in our mind verse for verse.

This time can't last forever, it will be over soon, and then comes the hard part, living life set free.

If I start to lose my focus or my grip, stand prepared for "part 2" of Mr. Pratt vs. Mr. D.P.

"Heat"

It can get so cold on these streets, that to stay warm you may need some heat.

Not the kind that controls the temperature, but the kind that rests under the driver's seat. Some like semi-automatics, but a revolver is best if you are forced to do dirt.

After you have handled your business you have two final steps to take to make it all work,

No.1, leave no shells at the scene and wipe it all down and don't forget the trigger.

No. 2, break that thang down and let it rest at the bottom of the river. Guns don't hurt people; the truth is that people hurt guns.

When innocent kids and old folks die on these streets, I blame the shooter, he is the wrong one.

The average Afro-American male has already lost his constitutional right to bear arms, And WE are forced to depend on the same crooked cops that took BIG and Pac from their Moms.

Last night, I saw five cops, and these five cops carried five black Glocks.

On my block, those five cops licked off five shots and watched five young black male hearts come to a stop.

The moral of this story is to ask yourself, "are you a man or are you a mouse?"

This heat that I pack is by force, not by choice, because I can only depend on me to protect this house.

"Time Won't Wait"

Everything that has happened to me, I could never change, it was just my fate. Life tends to run at high speed with no brakes and such is time, it just won't wait.

We seem to never have enough time during the day and don't expect this to ever change. Imagine running on borrowed time as it flies by and you switch in and out from lane to lane.

Many may never understand that for some of us time is in slow motion and at times it seems to completely cease.

As you whine and complain about bills and gas, try living in my world that's controlled by corrupt police.

Both our worlds are filled with snakes that spit venom that turns into uncontrolled hate

Because no one wants to bake it, but we all want the biggest piece of life's cake.

If I could give back yesterday in exchange for tomorrow, this would help to ease my mind.

I would substitute more of my life's simple times for the time I wasted on my grind.

Many times in this life of sin, we are blinded by the light that was given to guide our way.

Every man will realize either by choice or by force that time just won't wait.

"That Bag"

It goes by several names from a bag, to pack, or even a hood dope sack. When it's illegally sold, it is done either hand to hand or in a hood dope trap.

I'm talking to you dope boys, and if you are not one of them, then to you I am speaking Chinese. So many men have tried to conquer that bag and have been brought to their knees.

If you think that you know, then I don't think that you know, "Dude."

You just sealed your fate not knowing you sold that D.E.A. Agent that brick of dog food.

Many have said they're getting in and getting out, but that monster called greed will not let you quit.

And I'm sorry to inform you that your main man just added your name to a federal indictment. This criminal lifestyle you have chosen is full of fortune and luxuries that were obtained in a dangerous way.

When your P.S.I. comes back with those three prior felonies, you are looking to be sentenced to all day.

Realize that they are watching when you think they're not, and they will rumble through your trash.

If you are getting money, prepare to fall, and give all the thanks to that bag.

"Who's to Blame?"

I want to know who is to blame for my freedom being taken away.

I was never caught doing a crime but, I cannot fight what the government says. I want to know who is to blame for the constant bloodshed in the Middle East.

I fully realize that war makes money, and the bloodshed will not soon cease. I want to know who is to blame for our youth wanting to live life like Jezzg,

They do not understand the drug deals and gang wars he faced, and his bread did not come easy. I want to know who is to blame for this country's outrageously high debt.

Bush is on his way out of office, and he is trying to get all the cash he can get.

I want to know who is to blame for the murders of Biggie and Pac.

These corrupt cops played a major role in both deaths so when will the lying stop?

I want to know who is to blame for the tragedy that happened on September eleventh,

While Bin Laden raised hell and so many innocent Americans went to heaven.

There are too many questions that require too many answers for my topics of the day.

These questions demand to be answered to find out exactly where the blame must lay.

"Cut Your Grass"

Your life is like your lawn, you must keep it on the low. Many of your so-called friends are your foes. I'm telling you this in love, and hope you escape the fall.

You won't be able to see these snakes if your grass grows too tall. We all have fallen victim to the ones we kept the closest.

So don't let your guard down again, and continue to stay focused.

Be very cautious about who knows your business, it is not for public discussion, you may be talking to one, but watch those boys who are ear hustling.

The cowards act like women and refuse to be a man.

If there is any weakness shown they will corrupt your master plan. You will realize your demise if you are extremely cautious and lucky.

Those that claim their friends to the end are out for blood like Chucky. That one guy you know who tends to ask too many questions,

He will try to cut you the deepest and help to keep you stressin'. It has always been saying for you to keep your enemies close,

A lot of your enemies are your friends, and they can hurt you the most. The moral of this teaching is in hopes that all pass,

You may never know what is in your yard if you never cut your grass.

"Time Doing You"

When you are stuck in a 14'X7' cell, then you will know this to be true. No matter how long these folks give you, never let that time do you.

So many of us have been taken away, and I am speaking of "we" young black males. Their unjust laws are forcing us into genocide, or a life sentence in a living hell.

We men need to be there for our families, to raise our sons with the vision to see that if you follow too close in my footsteps, you'll end up in here just like me.

We, as a race, must help all our children to win at this white man's game.

If we don't take the time to teach our kids, the outcome will remain the same.

It's so hard for our lovely women to make it out there all by themselves because their men are hiding behind bars for conspiracies and crack sales.

No, I am not a racist, but if you are then do what you do.

I fully understand who will suffer the most if that time starts doing you.

Dedicated to all young black Males stuck doing time.

"Cop A Plea"

I hope you now realize how good it feels to be free.

When you barely made a bond, man, you better cop yourself a plea.

These feds are not playing with you and the US Attorney said what he meant. Why wouldn't he mean what he said when his conviction rate is 99 percent.

I'm not telling you to roll over or even give up your man,

But if you choose to go to that box, be sure you fully understand. If the feds are forced to pay for you and your expensive trial, they will give you 400 months with a coke and with a smile.

I, too, have been faced with the biggest decision of my incredibly young life, Do I try these people in their court, and if so, at what price?

Your life is so valuable and it's the only one that you get,

That jury could care less about those kids you fed and this you can surely bet. If you believe in anything you better trust in God up above,

Cause if you take these people to trial, they guarantee to show you no love. I know what I'm saying if you walk in my shoes you will see,

That the quickest way home to your family is by coping yourself a plea.

"Out of Sight and Out of Mind"

We have so many friends who love us or so they say, but I'm not blind to the waving signs.

My lust for money put me in prison and my imaginary friends see I'm out of sight, so I'm out of mind.

Don't be taken by surprise because even your so-called best friend's back can also turn, but when we are living life and looking good there seems to be no need for concern.

I hope you don't take my advice lightly; I live with it daily in this hell called jail,

Those same friends and family you helped feed on the street, won't send you a dime and no mail.

I didn't bite my tongue, a family is what I said and for some of us they tend to treat you the worst,

When dealing with family, they push the knife in your back the deepest and that aggravates the hurt.

I will let you in on a secret, a lot of the people I call family don't even have my blood. I look at Dwayne and Fate as brothers and we are family, bonded by brotherly love. All your friends and family cannot be put in this clique of many clowns,

My mother continues to help keep me strong and Derson always holds me down. So, in conclusion, you must ask yourself, what can I count on in my worst of times?" Who would care that I'm gone or would I just be put out of sight and out of mind?

Dedicated to All those fair-weather friends

"Sucka Free"

The main key to remaining sucka free is to evaluate every member of your crew.

Always let your first mind guide you, if you won't listen to yourself then you're through.

Always keep your eyes wide open; you may be forced to keep them open in your sleep.

If you lose focus of your adversary, then the penalty for stupidity is defeat.

Sometimes, Guerilla tactics become necessary, and Pac taught us about "me and my girlfriend."

Certain suckas are overly aggressive, so your girl might have to ride to the bloody end.

My attitude toward these people has placed them in the same category as the police,

And, if you don't secure your camp's perimeter, no one will be allowed one moment of peace.

These are haters and suckas and they make up a large percentage of the no-good nigga section.

If you see one, you will know one, and you must stay alert for your protection.

In essence, believe nothing that you hear, and only half of what you see.

We must continue to be 100 with ourselves, and by any means remain sucka free.

"Finally, Free"!

My niggas and I are no longer in bondage or so this country wants us to believe.

Just because now our chains are made of platinum, please don't allow yourself to be deceived.

We must not continue to be victimized by debt, as we try to buy everything we see,

Make a stand on your own two feet and realize that only we can set ourselves free.

As a people, we make up such a small portion of this land, but we hustle without fear,

That same small portion we represent tends to spend more money than we make each year.

Real will recognize real no matter how it is camouflaged in these last days and times,

For our bodies to be set free, we must first learn how to free our minds.

There are so many brothers locked away for feeding their families the best way they could,

But instead of showing us a better way to eat, this corrupt system encouraged being no good.

We too want the finer things out of life, but our own lives we can't always save,

If we can save one life by getting our hands dirty, we either live in the past or rest in a grave.

I am the voice of my people that live in this hell on earth and that's not how it's supposed to be.

A few of us will have to die, but our deaths will allow so many others to finally be free.

"Pump Your Brakes"

So many lives have been destroyed by pumping pounds and baking cakes.

If I paid attention to the signs that said use caution and pumped my brakes.

The phrase 'pump your brakes' has been an intricate piece of our black dialogue,

It has been used as a synonym for many meanings and for problems this phrase solved.

To pump your brakes can have so many different and unorthodox pieces in between.

So, if I told you to slow down or to take your time, it would basically mean the same thing.

We all should be fully capable to realize when we need to take our fast-off lips' gas.

I hope you un-decode my hidden message and slow down before them people raid your stash.

We are by nature so very quick to talk and so remarkably slow to listen,

The answer to your problems could be in your face but if you talk too much, you will miss them. I have been told all my life that a soft behind is what a hard head makes.

Some of us will have to bump our heads while the smart ones simply pump their brakes.

"So Hard"

In certain situations, life will demand that we play our last trump card,

But if you do not know the last trump that life holds, it can make your decision so hard.

When these feds indict you and your folks their goal is to max out your charge,

I hope you know about the ten to twenty-year difference between soft and hard.

Stay out of the way and no one can say that you were perpetrating the fraud.

You must learn to watch your own back or that knife will go in it so hard,

Never let your right know what your left is doing, or you may begin to feel paranoid.

We must strike while the iron is hot and if we wait, success is made so hard.

Place your trust in one woman because more than one will leave you emotionally scarred.

That one woman must be your best friend to help ease the pain when times are so hard.

If you feel as though you cannot go on, you can only find peace in the Lord.

He is the only one who can ease your pain in this life that we have made so hard.

"Trust Must Be Earned"

If a man is cut deep enough, he may lose too much blood which he needs to survive, but in reality, many men pray for death and hope that this is his time to die.

We must slow down and pay close attention to the ones who surround us, they are our greatest worry.

Most of the time, we move at high speed through life and lose our focus recklessly in such a hurry.

Those who claim to be your friends must be asked, "what are the contents of our friendship?"

Is it this life in the lights or maybe those stash spots filled with cash and those expensive whips? I hope you know who you can and can't trust, understand me, it's a must that you know,

When he says he will take the weight for you, "is he for real" or just putting on a show.

These days, it pays to know if your friends are solid or will they run when times get thick.

Your enemies send she-devils to destroy you, so use the right head when dealing with that chic.

These lines you have read, I hope to burn into your mind because life is only what you make it.

So, don't believe what you hear and half of what you see, it's your life to live, so stand up and take it.

We go through many stages of life and every stage is a lesson that you must learn.

For the ones I do trust, I never gave it to you, because over time, my trust was earned.

"That's Just the Way It Is"

Many of our children are dying and their mothers are crying far too many tears.

I wish it would all stop, but I know it won't and that's just the way it is.

If we all could feel the pain felt by one of our mourning sisters or brothers,

We would all develop a full understanding and realize that only we can help one another.

The gap between life and death must be closed to see the beginning come to an end.

So, if your man takes a shot to the face in your place, then he was truly your friend.

Most of us have fair-weather friends but don't see it until thin gets thick.

At that point and time, it's too late to evaluate and now you are the one left feeling sick.

The ones that think they know are the ones that don't have a clue,

Never lose track of who you are and what you are because only you can take care of you.

As my life slowly comes to an end, I finally can see that the lust for power can kill.

I have learned my lesson and thank God for His blessings and I see that's just the way it is.

"Mr. Accident"

In this country's years of glory, we have been led by many great presidents.

But now, this country's collective heart is barely beating, thanks to Mr. Accident.

Let us think back to his first four-year term and the mistake made in Florida,

Do you think he won the election or was it because his brother was Governor?

In his victory for his second term, was fraudulent and was only two years ago.

Mr. Accident was given the win by a miscount in Ohio.

Our Mr. Accident has our nation in an unnecessary war.

During the nine eleven tragedy, the Bid Laden family flew out of the U.S., and who knows what for?

Mr. Accident has put our country in its largest deficit, and it without a doubt affects our nation's poor.

We bombed Iraq and now we're rebuilding it, the word stupid tends to come up more and more.

The U.S. has spent millions overseas when many single mothers can't pay their rent,

What more proof do we need to realize voting for this clown was a huge accident.

Lady Liberty is a lady liar and there is no truth in her.

She ignored the cries for help in New Orleans when it was destroyed by Katrina. We are faced with record gas prices as we wait for the oil chokehold to loosen.

Mr. Accident's family is in the oil business, as they get paid, we get no solution.

All I can say is if the U.S. elects another accident, it will cost us it all,

We need a president that will stand on his word or surely divided we shall fall.

"No Love"

Do you know how it feels to be treated as though you do not exist?

As if the world was playing favorites and you somehow did not make its list?

For you to gain an advantage, you may be forced to push and shove.

But never expect for the road to be easy because this world will show no love.

What I am trying to say is, if you don't comprehend or already know,

Is that what you get you must earn, and sometimes this process is slow.

There is nothing in life for free except for dreams and prison time,

Since I know you do not want to be in prison, I hope your dreams will relax your mind.

When you begin to have faith in someone is when your heart is usually crushed.

Therefore my faith will remain in the Lord, and my life has been spiritually touched.

In this life, you must concentrate on what it is and not on what it was.

You should never give up on yourself and prepare to be shown no love.

"In the Struggle"

Life is broken down into pieces, and there are several to make up the puzzle.

That same life is the only one you get, so prepare to be in the struggle.

If you were not born with a silver spoon, then you must know how it feels to be black, I speak for America's young black males who are constantly under attack.

If we are not killing one another, these crooked police will take up the slack. They would love to see us all dead in coffins, looking up while flat on our backs.

Think of someone other than yourselves, when our children are caught in the mix, we are blind and only see one way out and that is by flipping pounds and bricks.

It has been hard on our people for over 400 years, and it is up to us to make it change.

If we never choose to stand together, we will continue to fall for anything.

There are so many of us that have no chance, and life forces us to hustle.

No one wants to be denied a chance, but it remains hard for us in the struggle.

Section Two

Growth From Pain

"Look into My Eyes"

When you look into my eyes, can you tell me exactly what it is that you see?

Do I scare you or make you nervous by the animal that you see inside of me?

I've looked into my mirror and the man I see looking back at me seems to be insane.

What I see and what you see cannot be the same because you see hope while all I see is pain.

My Father, the Creator of all, must have made His first mistake by blowing into my lungs breath, or did my Father make a bad decision by not putting me inside of a condom made of latex?

For your good, I advise you not to look into my eyes for a prolonged time.

These eyes that you stare into are filled with fury and my rage may erupt with no warning sign.

Maybe, if I no longer existed, who would mourn? Hell, most of the time, I don't love me.

Death is at times, my closest friend, and my occasional lover whose very presence sets my mind free.

For you to feel a man's pain, you must first travel the road he has traveled.

You may soon realize that you have no idea how he feels and left wondering why he used both barrels.

I plead with you for one last and final time; please listen to those who make no sound when they cry.

If you want to feel a portion of my pain, you need only to look into my eyes.

"May I Please Rest"

Inside of my mind, I am not allowed a moment's rest in this life. My life is a never-ending and unyielding psychological test I have yet to pass, but I know not one before me that has slain this beast, so I continue to press on in anticipation of my future happiness and peace.

If I were granted the chance to rewind time, I would change only the vision of my past, never my path itself for the path that was taken made me a man, not just an adult nor a mere grown-up, but most importantly a real man.

I would never substitute those so-called "friends" who left me for dead, or the ones who thought they were playing games with my head, you were my greatest inspiration, without you, I would have never grown, but by now, you cowards are fully known.

As I look back on my life, I've lived beyond others' expectations, but not my own, never my own. My young seeds, whose hearts I have selfishly broken, to you I apologize, and to you only. You never asked to come to this world. I made that choice for you and then left you freezing in this cold, cold world. I am ashamed of my actions and beg for your forgiveness, we were children growing up together from a distance. I did not realize this until you were children no more. Of my many mistakes, this, I assure you, was my greatest of all. I have used this pen as a sword to try to cut away this pain from my heart, I now ask with the purest humility, "Now may I please rest?"

"Solo"

The journey I am on was meant for me to learn how to grow. Although I have my family in my eyes, my mission is strictly solo.

There is always a lesson being taught and you must recognize the professor. We may not want to be taught, but hopefully, the next time, we'll know better.

Being alone can be one man's paradise, but for another, his doorway to the house of pain. You may need to be by yourself to find yourself, only then can you appreciate the change. Fear rules the minds of the lonely even if the lonely are not alone.

Stand and face your fear, the sooner you do, the loneliness shall be gone. Living life is not always easy and it's even harder when you're by yourself. In this case, reach deep within, there is where most courage is kept.

Have faith in God and yourself, for this rain will allow your seed to grow.

We can make it through the pain and with God's love we never really did it, Solo.

"Carried by Six"

When my time here is over, my soul must find rest in Heaven or eternal torture in hell.

I pray to my Father that I don't pass in my sleep in the unworthy jail cell.

After I'm gone, I hope my light shined bright, I believe that it did as I recollect.

I have lost my life to this world, but my afterlife holds divine respect.

Some children have had to bury a parent and some parents have had to bury a child,

I still can see my grandmother's soul and would love to just talk to her for a while.

In death, our burdens are light where in life they were so very heavy.

The family you left behind lives in pain and for this type of situation, they could never be ready.

I was foolishly willing to give my life for useless riches and hitting licks,

Therefore, in an instant, you must choose to be judged by twelve or to be carried by six.

In essence, we were all born to die, so fear not, for this was understood from the very start,

Tomorrow is not promised, so tell your loved ones how you care and what you feel in your heart.

Live every day like it's your last, life is the lottery that you have already hit.

Death is impossible to beat and no matter, right or wrong, you will one day be carried by six.

"Tales from My Hood"

It is all real in my hood, because it's either life or death on these cold streets. Only put faith in God and yourself because these niggas will kill to eat.

If you have held the hand of heartache and seem to stay in the presence of pain,

A young boy searches for attention from his alcoholic dad but finds love in the Crips street gang.

There is a beautiful little girl who wants her crack fiend mother's love and affection.

That little girl in now pregnant at 13 from her mother's brother molesting her without protection.

It may seem to be no love in this mini-Vietnam that I call my hood.

Outsiders only see drug deals and gun play but look a bit deeper if you would.

There are small babies playing in these streets so slow down for the bumps and watch the signs,

I hope you feel what I say, because your hood is no better or worse than mine.

Many of us thank God daily to still be breathing and that is a natural fact.

A lot of those that make it out the hood, step on that gas and never look back. This is a slap in the face to your friends and relatives that are still there.

Never forget the hood that raised you and let the ones still stuck know that you care.

The picture that I have painted for you is all real and I pray that it is understood.

So many of us have been tried by fire from the lessons we learned from the hood.

"Pain"

We all have lost someone we love to that beast we all call pain.

I am writing to you to help you get through in hopes that it is not in vain.

Some of us will take the easy route to try and stop all our pain

By taking a razor and slitting our wrist and watching as our blood starts to drain.

Many will use that nine double "M", the one with the seventeen shots.

To find out once and for all, will one shot make the pain stop?

Some of us plunge into the pool of life and always at the deepest end, knowing that pain will not let us focus, plus, we never learned how to swim. You play the cards that life has given you, no matter how bad the deal,

But some of us just can't take the pain and take a fistful of sleeping pills. We must all face our maker on that day that is unknown still.

A coward will give in to the pain; it takes a real man to continue to live.

I am hoping you can understand my message and can see that I am right,

Because I have walked up on death's doorstep, and tried taking my own precious life. In that region in our minds, we must learn to conquer life's crazy game.

I am not afraid to die, but I am wondering why I cannot get rid of all this pain.

"Pain"

Without question, we have all lost a loved one to the beast by the alias name of pain.

I am writing to you all to help you through this life into the next and keep you all sane.

It's unavoidable that some of us will take the easiest route to try and stop all of our pain,

By taking a razor and slitting your wrist and watching as your blood slowly starts to drain.

Some will pick up the .357 you know that magnum, the one with those six hollow-tipped shots, to find out once and for all, will one shot make all the pain stop.

Many will plunge into the pool of worry and despair and always at the deepest end, knowing full well the pain will not allow you to focus, plus you never learned how to swim. We must play the cards that life dealt us, no matter how bad the deal.

But some will continue to run from the pain and hide behind a fistful of sleeping pills.

We all must stand face-to-face with our maker on what day is unknown still.

Remember a coward will give his life to pain, and it takes a real man to be strong enough to live.

I hope that you comprehend my message and realize what I say to be right.

Because I have knocked on death's door and tried to give up on my own precious life.

In that region of our minds, we see that life is an ongoing series of mental games.

I have no fear to die, but I'm left wondering why I can't eliminate all of my pain.

"Losing Control"

The medication that has been prescribed for me seems to no longer help to control me.

There is no one here that I can trust no matter how hard they try to get to know me.

I just want my life back, and I want people to stop asking me "what's wrong?"

The best solution for what I want would have been for me to have stayed at home.

I gave up my right to make that decision such a long time ago.

My mind is lost like I'm in a mental maze and Lord knows I can't take too much mo.'

Reaching out for my sanity is comparable to me reaching out for a star.

Understanding that survival is a must, no matter what or where you see.

It is hard to realize that being a manic depressant keeps me digging myself a deeper hole.

I really feel more like a psychotic deranged lunatic on the verge of losing control.

The help that I need cannot be given by a man or any mere human being.

If you have ever felt like death was your only true friend, then you know exactly what I mean.

Never forget who you are no matter how much pain, pressure, and disappointment you are forced to face.

You can make it through any trial or tribulation with God's help and His never-changing grace.

"Stuck in the Middle"

This life I lead can be so unpredictable and at times, fell like a gigantic riddle.

Instead of becoming simpler to beat, I seem to continue to be stuck in the middle.

We must all prepare ourselves for life's ups and downs, and those dreaded twists and turns.

As we continue to grow we learn to accept life strictly on life's terms.

The people we trust and depend on are the ones that seem to hurt you the most.

Let that be a lesson learned, for their negative actions constitute keeping them close.

Many of us realize that the word "family" really only means we share the same blood, because there are so many that are not our "family" and they tend to show us the most love.

There are morals to all stories, but it's up to you to realize and try to understand.

The world loves to tell you that you can't, but you must find the strength to know that you can.

Allow your life to be a gift to yourself, because to so many others, it will mean so little. Always live your life outside the box or be doomed to remain stuck in the middle.

"Two Pretty Colors"

There are so many beautiful colors, so many shades, but today, I will only discuss two.

These are the colors of war, and they, of course, are "dead" red and "true" blue.

If you wondered why these colors create a passion for death, look no further than "your" American flag.

Today, young Black and Latino males will only pledge allegiance to the truth, that .357 or .44 mag.

So many young boys look for love in the same arms that hold war machines such as M-16s and AK47s.

The same love that his mom shows for crack, he's never met his dad, and that's why he has been bangin' since 11.

Too many hearts have stopped beating from the savage warfare these two colors can and will ignite.

In our urban areas these battles are uncontrollable, and some of the innocent fell victim in these bloody gun fights.

This country could care less about the constant death of our youth that make up both sides.

Why would white America care about our young, when they want to sign them off in the blood of genocide.

I, too, must be held accountable for my role in the destruction of my own black brothers. Now that I'm older, I was a fool to trade gunfire and be driven insane over a simple color.

So, choose this day life or death, to be blessed or cursed and take full responsibility for what you do.

I no longer practice this lifestyle but will have an endless connection to the colors of red and blue.

"No Place to Run"

When your enemy has infiltrated your mind, how much help is that gun?

Unless it is used to blow your brains from you head, you have no place to run.

Many try to hide behind drugs, alcohol, and cheap sexual thrills.

Realizing too late an overdose, drunk driving, and that package all can kill.

Living life at high speed is so foolish, but it takes years for you to understand.

We try to grow up too fast in such a rush to be what the world calls a man.

Treat life like you are not getting another one because this is a known fact.

When you leave this world, only reincarnation can bring you back.

If you have a loving family, show them love back daily, they deserve it all.

Unconditional love does not cost a dime, but it becomes priceless every time that we fall.

Be there for the ones who love you the most and for me his name is Derson.

I have been taught by heartache with family beside you, we need no place to run.

"Training Day"

Do not try to run from the desert eagle and not talking for there is nothing for you to say.

I am delighted to welcome you to your first day of class or better yet, your first training day.

There must be an adjustment of our first session for me to keep the peace.

If you refuse my training, this gun against your head will fry your waves and melt the grease.

Lesson No. 1; keep your hands in plain view, until we get to that part of class.

I have taught many classes with hours of training either with or without this mask.

Lesson No. 2; never force me to raise my voice I would prefer if we continue to whisper.

Let us not forget about your lovely wife, if we run into issues, my trigger will softly kiss her.

For your final lesson of the day, I must learn what you really value the most.

If it is you and your wife continuing to breathe, then today's training is done and I'm ghost.

You must know by now that you were trained by the best and there will not be another above me.

In your first training day you learned how a family survives a cunning armed robbery.

Straight Jackise'!

"Mind Control"

Inside this place of pain, where the sun seems to never shine,

Keeping your sanity is a must, as so many want you to lose it, if they cannot control your mind.

We must realize and take full advantage of our opportunities there shall be so few.

What allows my mind to be free may serve no purpose or significance for you.

The average person views life from the third person and frequently sits and observes himself. As we sit and watch with no emotions, being non-emotional destroys our dreams and dooms us to fail.

The biggest myth tied to mind control is that one can change or control another's mind. This theory has been proven to be accurate, but we still try to make another change and we are making time.

Let us look at a child who grows up all alone, who wants friends, but is still all by himself. As he grows into an adult, he develops an alter ego who fights his battles when extreme pressure is felt.

In essence, the mind is the trigger of the gun of life, and every thought is a shot that must explode.

"Never Change"

I have been bruised and beaten by the stick of life and for some reason this beating does not feel strange.

Through my life I have been extremely disobedient and felt I could never change.

As I live my life looking into my own window of misfortune and my many mistakes made,

I am still breathing regardless of my stupidity and lack of self-control and a large price was paid.

This world we share can turn a baby into a leader of many nations if he is only taught.

That same world can change that baby into a murderous monster that somehow must be caught.

Change is a word that most will not accept unless its process is totally pain free.

But anything that is worth having, is, at times painful, please take this from me.

We are always so afraid to use the word never even if it is meant from our heart.

If you find yourself frightened by this word and you want to grow, you have just found your start.

Are you really satisfied with yourself, or are you just lying to the one who must stay true?

There is no one who can hold you down, except the one in your mirror, yes, you.

Always keep your view on life crystal clear and oh so real and plain.

When you're stuck in front of the gun with no place to run, you can no longer say that, "I will never change."

"Dying Inside"

My adversary has taken from me my most precious attribute which is my pride.

In war, as in love, all lips will lie, deceit is poison and once taken, prepare to begin dying inside.

This assailant that I speak of is without doubt my savage alter ego known as "myself".

So, he knows all my secret battle tactics and the ways in which my most excruciating pain is felt.

I have pled with my Father to spare me and take away my other and allow me to be whole again.

But Satan himself calls me by name, saying, "My child, enjoy this pain, for I am your only friend."

This cruel world in which I live seem to be a fantasy or nightmare filled with torment and pressure.

Mine enemy fills my thoughts with "The Scarlet" and my weak flesh forces me to mentally undress her.

As I search for an answer to my question, "Why must I suffer in this hell on earth?" My life was given to me as a gift that has somehow been transformed into a curse.

Like a fool, I stand prepared for more sorrow that can only be taken away by my own suicide.

This decision is made in search of eternal peace and to take away my agony caused from dying inside.

"Blood In, Blood Out"

I will never pledge allegiance to any country or to any flag.

My allegiance is pledged to God and myself, as I pull and bust this .44 mag.

In this war in which I fight daily, I am a soldier and shall never cry nor pout.

Mine enemy shall never surrender so this war calls for blood in and blood out.

These blocks are our battle fields, and many of our troops are too young to be drafted,

As we prepare for casualties of war, there is no preparation for a fourteen-year-old in a casket. For you to feel what I feel, in the trenches in where we must meet,

Many soldiers have been crucified by these courts, so now we hold court in these streets.

The alliance between comrades should be infinite, but some become cold-hearted enemies.

There seems to be no loyalty among thieves and knowing this to be is the key for me.

This cruel world rest in her final stages it like the beginning of the battle of "Armageddon."

I hope and pray that someday all my sins are forgiven and I can open that door into heaven. This war shall rage until it's finished and my friends in this, I have no doubt.

Christ spilled his innocent blood for us to get in, and we must spill our own to get out.

"Revenge"

Whenever you feel as though you have been violated especially by family or friend,

Your mind without hesitation goes into defense mode that calls for immediate revenge.

Revenge is a serious word though it may be small; it can mean the difference between life and death.

There must be complete caution used in this issue or you may end up hurting yourself. Some say that there is no taste sweeter than the taste of revenge.

Revenge is a dish best served cold for your enemy to fully comprehend. In the Bible the Lord clearly says, "That any and all revenge is mine",

But for most of us we will not obey His law, because that vengeance comes in God's time.

Any eye for an eye may not be the solution you desire, or you may go blind.

If you lose sight of your problem, you may lose your sight as well as your mind.

Life is so very precious, if you could only ask one who lost theirs to the insanity.

Any action I take be it good or bad, can never judge my complete man or my humanity.

We all have been persecuted in this life, but we continue to breathe now until our end.

To secure success when this world hid it from you, is without a doubt, the sweetest revenge.

"Who's Got Yo' Back?

In these days and times, the young black male is under a constant attack.

As in the case of any endangered species, we must confide in those who have our back.

This corrupt government continues to set us up to do nothing but fail,

And we don't see their devious plan until we either die in the streets or doing life in jail.

We have become our own worst enemy as black on black murders are now the norm.

Our babies come into a world where they are unwanted and later wonder why they were even born.

This country wants us to become non-existent, so our race can no longer reproduce.

If America had its way, our people would vanish through genocide and enslave the rest like "Roots".

Black man, go back to your homes, raise your sons, without us our families will die.

There are too many black gays and federal inmates that sisters are forced to give Y-T a try.

I hope you understand the importance of my message, black men are proud to be black.

My life belongs to Christ and there is a family of Pratts that got my back.

"Crystal Clear"

Could you imagine a world without pain, sorrow, or even fear?

This society would reign supreme if only our view was crystal clear.

At certain periods in our lives, what we see may not make sense.

But anything that does not come out in the wash surely comes out in the rinse.

Every individual possesses a treasure that is valued beyond their life,

That treasure could be your child, your husband, or maybe even your wife.

We are all born dying that has been understood from our birth.

If you are prepared to give your life, be sure you get all it's worth.

When our vision is impaired by our wrong decisions and such,

That crystal-clear vision that we persist to seek means so very much.

Our hearts direct us to walk, but this world tells us to run.

We must learn to defend ourselves with our minds and not with guns.

There is no place to hide in a world made of glass and mirror.

Always hit life head on, and your view will stay crystal clear.

"Death Before My Ink Dries"

These words that speak so loud from this paper in which it has been written, If I have hurt a heart or smashed a soul, may my faults be forgiven.

There is a message in every word I write, and power comes from its simple recital,

My verses have been created to continue to live when I die and standalone by its very title.

In this world in which we live, none of us can or will continue to live forever,

But until I take my last breath, I will fight tooth and nail and surrender never.

I say to you this day, take life by its reigns and continue to tame this savage beast.

Your problems and futile conflicts of this life are viewed as transparent at the very least.

We must find a way to continue to move forward when it's so very easy to stop.

There are many future generations who will need our guidance to direct them to the top.

This passage has been written to correct any deception, deceit, and any soul I blinded by lies.

I give you my soul in preparation of my death before my ink starts to dry.

"Frustration"

There are days that roll by swift, but they usually slide by slow.

Every day is a frustrated struggle if you live in a cage like me you already know. All of us are searching for the key to open the lock.

Time will not pass fast if you continue to watch that clock. In this world of trouble, we all need to search for salvation.

While our leader has started this war then he went on vacation. I refuse to defend a country that would never fight for me.

So, give me freedom or give me death, my choice is so easy.

There is no way to predict life's lessons; there are constant twists and turns. But today, the price we pay will force us to live and learn,

I wish the world was all beautiful like a star up in the sky. Do not be a fool, which is my first rule to never live a lie.

Most of us living in this concrete hell; we are forced to practice patience. I am just a man who will extend his hand for help with my frustration.

"Simple"

We are all given the same understanding which has always been 90% mental.

But some of us continue to make life hard when it's supposed to be so simple.

Just like a small child who plays in his pen with many Lego blocks,

They send young black men to the pen for playing around with birds and glocks.

This world in which we live can either make you or break you,

And the choices that we made in our past tend to hinder our mental breakthrough.

As a youth, I was told to K.I.S.S. – keep it simple stupid my son.

I tried with all that was in me, but I still seem not to get it done.

Make sure that you don't complicate your life; the world will reserve that job.

Some of us can open life's doors, while others can't even touch the knob.

When we make it hard on ourselves, some will choose to put that nine to their temple.

If we would just open our eyes and come to realize that life really could be so simple.

"If You Try Me!"

Everybody nowadays is looking for something for free even if they gotta take it.

You may never know the corruption in a man's heart, look into his eyes they can't fake it.

This life is so hard, but if it comes down to me or you, I feel for your family.

Black on black is not my first option, but if you push me, my hammer falls randomly, and when I blast, I'm forced to empty my strap, and your cap is quickly peeled back.

I wish it could have been another way, but I can't allow you to retaliate from my attack.

Your kids have lost their father in a matter of seconds due to your total ignorance.

Because you made a fatal error in trying me, now you are only thought of in the past tense.

The moral of this lesson is to warn you about my kind and you need to open your eyes and see,

Just watch your mouth and protect your neck, it could cost you big if you ever try me.

I wish it didn't have to be this way, but this is the way you made it to be.

Never take your life for granted, son, these multiple shots just set your mind free.

"F_ _ _ k The World"

I hate this muthaf_ _ _ _a and I can tell this muthaf_ _ _ _a hates me.

While stuck in this frame of mind and through bloody eyes I can't see.

If I could kill every one of them, that would be my one and only wish,

This place has poisoned my mind, and I await death's fatal kiss.

You may think of it as murder, or is it just my lack of speech? Does anybody really give a damn, or am I just walking dead on my feet? I want to be rid of this feeling that may cause me to take a pure life.

The words that I have put on this paper seem to cut deep as a knife.

I have tried to regain my piece of sanity that allows me to maintain,

But there is a voice that rings in my head asking me, "Do you enjoy the pain?"

I have given up on living this life and I stand ready for it to be over.

With so much hate taking over my heart, this weight is too heavy for my shoulders. The misery that rests in my mind will continue to gleam like a precious pearl.

This life is full of sh_t, let death come quick, as I scream out, "F_ _k the World!!!"

Dedicated to: People stuck in the headlock of the Struggle

"Dead"

In an instant, your breathing has stopped, and you lay flat in a puddle of red.

No matter how hard you try not to be, you now realize that you are dead.

As your soul hovers over the body that at one time was its home,

You hear everyone crying and others lying as you envision yourself as being gone.

Your life was taken away from you, and now God will be your only judge,

It is not yet fully understood, if you will go down below or rise above.

Your spirit is not the only one searching for answers to their many questions.

Just as you want to know they ask is it too late for one last holy blessing.

There is no doubt that it is too late for repentance for you wasted all your chances.

Your name is not written in the Lamb's Book of Life, and only you can be blamed for your circumstances.

As you begin to cry a pool of many tears, touching your face and wiping sweat from your head,

You now grasp that it was just a nightmare and you must find salvation before you are dead.

"A Bigga Nigga"

These lame-ass, so called hard cats can make you want to cock back that .45 and pull the trigga,

But when you know you just wasting a bullet, you must figga to be a bigga nigga.

It only takes for me to see the "Ho" in a man come out once and that's really plenty enough,

Because you already know when a nigga a "Ho" when his bitch is coaching him on talking tough.

I have met more than my share of these "instant gansta' type bitch niggas.

What I mean by "instant" is you just add water and then cut this "Ho" out with some scissors. Holding your peace and not using your piece on this coward can be so damn hard.

But when you know what you are dealing with it is a must to pull his cord. In the heat of the moment, you may have to "86" this bitch ass trick.

And, if he figga that he's bigga, then just digga a bigga ditch.

I really hope you won't be forced to show this "monkey" that he is fucking with a "Gorilla". Take that red dot off his head, cause he is the walking dead, and you are the "bigga nigga".

"Inside the Mind of a Serial Killa"

The evil that lives in my heart will only allow me to feel agony and pain,

As I fight against myself not to kill once more and now realize that I've gone insane.

With .45 ways to reach an evil orgasm in the palm of my hand this day I choose life. But as I try to resist death's temptation, my soul may be claimed this very night.

In my pursuit of peace, I would lay down my life if I was given the chance to start again,

I have contemplated self-murder, but my Father would never forgive an unforgivable sin.

I don't want to continue to cause others pain, or at least that's what my heart of stone continues to cry.

After the rush of my last murder, I now realize that I'm only telling myself another lie.

In the act of taking a life, you must cover all tracks for you to remain free.

I have no concern of being caught, and I will get them before they could ever get me.

There have been so many victims that I have saved from this painful hell on earth.

They were all judged accordingly and found guilty of living a life without worth.

I have painted the picture and it may sound like a novel or a suspense thriller,

But you have just been taken on a ride, deep inside the mind of a serial killa.

"Caught in Life's Storm"

There is no escape when you are caught in one of life's storms.

Get to higher ground when hurricane stress begins to form.

Life's storms have three stages, and it's not our choice to choose, you're going in, stuck in the eye, or finally coming through.

The winds of pain blow oh so hard against your very will. This is a storm that we all must face, and that is on the real. The tornado called worry will try to rip you apart.

Through this storm, you must be brave and continue to follow your heart.

The thunder of depression has an effect on each and every one.

Many loud claps will be heard, just be calm until they're done.

Hate is a storm that has a mighty rage of no equal.

It comes to affect all of us, not just certain types of people.

This passage was written as motivation, I hope it has done no harm. My goal is to help someone who is caught in one of life's storms.

"Taken by The Darkness"

In everyone's mind there lies a place that is kept totally secret and from this realm of thought, our conscience allows our mind to digest sinister illusions. You search for the reason why you have found yourself in this place mentally. In this place, there is only darkness, and as you attempt to find your way out of this maze of terror, your breathing becomes extremely difficult. The darkness you are in has now become alive. As you reach out your hands, you feel a face cold like ice, and then it vanishes into the abyss that is your mind, now your heart rate pounds inside your chest. You now realize that you are not alone, but who shares your thoughts? Every step you take plunges you deeper into the teeth of the darkness. You attempt to scream, but all sound has become a prisoner of your thoughts and cannot be heard. As paranoia sets in, you are blinded by the darkness, you walk into a wall but as you touch it, the walls become alive.

Your first thought is to run, but where? There is no end to the darkness, and now the darkness wants more than your mind, it wants your life! Death has called your name and refuses to be denied. The cold hands of the reaper clutch your neck and he squeezes until you are left lifeless. It is now time for your soul to reach its destination. Death took the form of the darkness and now that darkness has transferred you to your place in eternity. Are these horror-filled dreams or calm and subtle nightmares? No matter the case and none the less, your journey was inevitable. May your soul finally rest in peace.

Section Three

LIFTED BY LOVE

"Thank You"

Dear Mrs. Dorothy Pratt and Baby:

I am writing this to you, for you, and about you. Sometimes, we all must reach our bottom. That bottom for one may be the top for another. I have reached my bottom and just as it should be you two were there waiting for me to help me back to the top. Not long ago, I didn't love me, but yawl showed me how to love again and that love is everlasting. You took my heart and locked it away on your cloud where all angels keep their most prized possessions.

If I didn't have you to hold me up, I would surely fall and not have the strength or desire to carry on. I now know who lifts me up and carries me when I can no longer walk, our Heavenly Father, but the request was made by one of His own, you, Momma, and Baby. There will never be any words that could express my gratitude for the role you play in my life but let me try. "Thank you" for being my rock when the storms of life are raging. "Thank you" for all the unconditional love you give. "Thank you" for touching my heart of stone and allowing it to beat again. I just want to tell you "thank you" for helping me to believe in myself, believe in you, and believe in us.

Love Always, Derrick

"Nothing Is Bigger Than Us"

The love that's shared between us is far more than special, it could cause a heart to stop beating just to listen to the sweet symphony played by our love. Love is nothing without an arch enemy and every love has its own catalyst, ours just so happens to be time. The time that we've lost being apart will serve to make us as strong as the waves of the mighty sea, or our love will crumble beneath it at the first sign of fear or hardship. I will stand strong for the love; its very existence is of unparalleled importance to me. Can we share this common bond for a lifetime? It shall be my tireless prayer that this always be true. Our love can grow to be as big as we will allow it to be, or, if left unattended for it can and will, shrivel up and die, but again we must not allow it to do so. I will always love you, and ride to the bloody end, this love will allow the blind to see that there is nothing bigger than us.

"Like No Other"

Mom has always been there unconditionally from the gate right by my side.

She could never be confused with Bonnie, but she held me down when I acted like Clyde.

If God would only bless us with maybe two or even with three,

This woman that I speak of is Momma, and she's forever down with me.

Those so-called ride or die chic's are scared to die or ride and they're so overrated.

She can feel my pain just by hearing my voice and she always came and never hesitated.

I wish we all could feel the power of her everlasting love.

In one sense, she is as strong as a lion and next, she is as gentle as a dove.

When I think that I am right, she is always there to say, "Son, you are wrong."

In the eyes of my momma, I'll be her baby forever and she really means that long.

You must treat her with the ultimate respect because this queen is your mother.

She will never leave your side, or run and hide, and her love is like no other.

Dedicated to: Dorothy Pratt,
My "Momma"

"Daddy Is Gone" For Derson Pratt

The eyes of a child can show pain beyond their years.

Those same little eyes seem to make the biggest tears.

The understanding of a child is very easy to get,

And they hang on Daddy's every word and this you can bet.

In the mind of our little ones, what Daddy says is the law.

Daddy be careful about what they see, they never forget what they saw.

Children need both parents, but most must settle for one.

Momma alone can't make a man out of her only son.

If Daddy only knew what that child was going through,

He would make trips to the beauty shop, and all the ball games, too.

There are so many single mothers that are forced to sing the same old song.

When her child asks, "Where is my daddy?" she says, "Baby, your daddy is gone".

Dedicated to all the single mothers and their children

"Magic"

The way you make me feel can only be described by the word magic. That little twinkle in your eye when I touch your back or kiss your neck. The cute little way you turn your head to the side when you want my attention. The bond that we share is electric and takes my breath away with just one look into your beautiful brown eyes. Girl, from the day that we met, you have taken a piece of my heart, and now that we are away from one another, that piece that you own has begun to grow and beat all on its own. Our connection is as strong as the arms of Atlas or the back of Samson. I vow my love to you today, tomorrow, and forever, simply put, girl, you and I are magic.

"She Is . . . Mine"

She is the brightest and the most breathtaking star up in the heavens, and she is exceptionally exquisite to the eye. She is the ray of sunlight that burst through the clouds and illuminates my day. She is most beautiful when she is all natural like the nectar of a sweet flower that is too irresistible for the bee to allow it to pass. She is that warm blanket on that cold winter night that wraps around you and makes you so content, warm and secure. She is that last shot of Remy Martin X.O straight with no chaser that tastes on your lips keeps you coming back for more.

She is that soft and gentle stream that flows silently down the mountain and her grace is beyond measure. She is that first stunning snowfall that covers the earth, and you lay in her bosom and she intensifies your obsession with her. She is that mighty thunderstorm that requires you to become so silent and calm until she passes you by and permits you to experience tranquility once more. She is the soft and subtle beach we run upon barefooted with not a care in the world and we roll on her as we make passionate love throughout the night. The finest way for me to describe to you what she is to me . . . Is that she is mine.

"Love Is Like A Diamond"

Some foolish people underestimate the power of love, in my past, I was one. Now, I fully respect its power as real love can sparkle like a diamond.

Baby, you are my sun and my shine in the thunderstorm called my life.

I am so fortunate to have you to lean on and blessed by you being my wife.

In my past, I have held in all my pain and that presence emotionally shut me down.

I stupidly dove into the sea of dismay and Sonya, my angel, refused to let me drown.

Our past verbal disputes began to test our love, and those tests seem to cause us problems. Then Jesus stepped in and whispered "love one another" then said, "I am your problem solver.

In essence, what I am trying to say is that without you, there could be no me.

As we continue to share our world as one and realize that the diamond of love is free.

"What Is Love?"

Many have pondered the question, "what is love?" Love is that euphoric feeling that overtakes you when the room feels as though it has been set ablaze by the embrace of that one person you would give your life for to be with them if only for a season. Love is when your eyes meet and you have plunged into the sea of romance in search of your Atlantis, as you go deeper. So deep until your breath is seized from your body.

Love is when you just touch that special someone and the pure ecstasy and anticipation of a simple kiss activates your bodies into an inferno, and you are drenched with sweat as you both sit in a room made of ice. Love is that time in your day when you know that all of your emotional energy will be concentrated into one hour, minute, or even one second which is needed to satisfy your hunger for love. Love is watching the world pass you by in the arms of an angel that has carried you away to paradise in your mind, in your heart, and your soul. Love is never asking "how can I, or why do I feel this way". You are engulfed in the flames of passion when you are merely in the presence of love.

Love, in essence, can take you so high that you are looking down at the moon and the stars, and true love is genuine, unconditional and will go unchanged until the end of time. That is what love is…Baby, can you feel me?

"Daddy's Baby Girl"

I have thought so much about you, but you're yet to enter my world.

You don't even have a name for now, so we'll just call you 'your Daddy's baby girl'.

Thoughts of me holding you in my arms seem to fill my heart with joy.

There is nothing that I won't do for my baby but Lord, please not another boy,

Daddy will buy you dolls and we'll play house, to me it's all the same.

And Daddy will give all thanks to God, because from His hands is where you came.

As you start school, I will drop you off, and I'll be right there to pick you up.

While you will like Mommies' car, you will love to be in your daddy's truck.

I'll even learn how to braid your hair and put in all those bows, ties, and twists, and if Daddy hurts his baby girl, I will apologize to you with a kiss.

Our talk about boys is quite a way off, because you can't have one until you are twenty-three.

But if you find one that we both like, the deciding vote still belongs to me.

For now, you only exist in my dreams and to me; you're more precious than any diamond or pearl.

I will always be here awaiting your arrival as your Daddy's baby girl.

Dedicated to my future daughter

"One"

This woman is everything to me. By night she is my moon, and by day, she is my sun.

There is no doubt about my love for her and that infinite love connects us as one.

I feel like a schoolboy who has become star struck by his first taste of puppy love.

This sensuality that I feel is no schoolboy crush, she is a gift from up above.

It is electric when her body touches mine; it feels as though we unite.

This woman is my soul mate, and I feel so sick when she is out of my sight.

There are only two words that can describe how she makes me feel and they are "at peace". My heavenly father has blessed me with an angel and for this gift His work I must keep.

Every man needs a special woman, one that he would give his life to protect.

Many men will search for her throughout eternity and for them I have remorse and respect.

I am so grateful to have found my queen and my young prince by the name of Derson. This woman has crowned me her King and we shall reign forever together as one.

"HER"

Dear Ms. You,

What does the word "special" mean to a man that has done everything? "Special" is that one woman that makes him complete and turns all of his frowns upside down. What does the word "ecstasy" mean when you have touched euphoria in its purest form? "Ecstasy" is so much more addictive that a drug. It's where she sends him every time he looks into her eyes.

What is "time" to him when it seems to stop with just one kiss from her sweet lips? "Time" starts again after that sweet taste of her lips has finally left his tongue. What is "space" to one that has all of it at his constant beckon call? It must be where they travel to as one when their bodies are locked in a fairytale type splendor.

Finally, what is "forever" to one that knows that life can never last that long? Without a doubt, this is the most colossal promise that has ever been made and he made it to her for eternity.

In essence, she is so "special" to him that for him to speak her name gives his mouth such sweet "ecstasy". He wants her to have all his "time." They want to share the same "space" be it inner or outer. They own one another's hearts now and "forever". I finally realize the answer to these questions has always simply been "You" and "Me". Love always, Mr. Me.

"Just for Now"

Time, I have begged to stop, and once again, I've been denied today.

In your loving arms, upon your breast, is where I wish my head to lay.

I can truthfully declare that you have always been my better half. Beyond the shadow of a doubt that is my reply for anyone who might ask. We never had everything, and for you it had meant even less.

If I could only rewind time, I would have listened to you, this I must confess.

Our Heavenly Father will give us back to one another and I know he knows how.

I anticipate our reuniting which is etched in my mind and is only a dream "Just for Now".

Section Four

INSPIRATION FOUND

"My Hero"

I could never put into words what you really mean to me.

But I will do my best and hope that I can help you see.

You have been more than my father; you have always been my friend.

I used to think you were hard on me, for your rules I tried to bend.

It seems like you were rough on me, but it was all part of your plan.

To change me from a hard-headed boy, into a full-grown man.

We wasted so many years being too tough to show our love.
We both are wiser and realize, it's okay for men to hug. You went out of your way for me, and that I will never forget.

The love I have for you is from my heart and is 100% legit.

If I had never known you, my understanding of love would have been gone. You are the strongest man I have ever known, and you will always be my hero.

Dedicated to Herbert Pratt (My Father)

"Life Without You"

I could not imagine my life without you. Countless times you and you alone stood by my side when so many others turned against me and showed me their backs. You are my angel of comfort always watching, caring, teaching, and loving. You are so true and so worthy of the title of my Mother. You were blessed with a smile that could electrify the entire sky. You have been the one and only devoted one in my life and no woman on earth could take your place in my heart, not even a wife. When I think of you, my thoughts are full of love and are simply flawless. You are the greatest gift that my Heavenly Father has ever blessed me to possess. There are no words that could begin to truly describe what you mean to me. I believe deep down in my heart that I would not be alive today if not for your love and God's unchanging grace. One day without your love, to me, would feel like an eternity alone in outer space, with every star that shines bright being a constant reminder of your beautiful face. Momma, if I was granted one wish, and one wish alone, it would be for you to live in my heart infinitely as you have been all the days of my life. I could never imagine, nor would I want to continue living this life without you.

Dedicated to my Momma

"Taken for Granted"

We as a people seem so shallow and our youth are in a struggle to understand it.

I feel their pain because it is mine and they can no longer be taken for granted.

If we could only be taught how to love as fast as we are taught how to hate,

Our troops in the Middle East would be at home, instead of the bewilderment of their fate.

The teachers that spend more time with our children than any of us as it stands,

They should be among the country's highest paid, as our futures rest in their hands.

The destiny of a nation rests in the hands of one man and I personally can't stand it.

This country should be a true democracy and stop taking its people's opinions for granted.

There are millions of dollars spent annually for the housing of inmates and this is pitiful.

Our taxpayers are told that prison is for convict rehab, but it just makes a more cunning criminal.

Use your head for more than a hat rack is what I was taught at a young age.

And we must all realize that every so-called animal is not always meant to be locked in a cage.

My message is simple, straight-forward, and to you in the raw is how it must be handed.

Life is a series of good and bad choices and neither of the two should ever be taken for granted.

"What If?"

What if every blind person woke up this morning realizing that he could see?

Would they just take a miracle for granted, or would they bow down on bended knee?

What if every white person was to unexpectedly be transformed into black?

Now, who would suffer from racial profiling and fall victim to Rodney King type attacks?

What if every homeowner was to help a family that was homeless?

Then that homeless family could proudly say, "Thank God for this home and we're blessed to own this."

What if it was possible for you to be in two places at one time?

With one of you being home with the family, and the other you block bleeding on the grind.

What if the United Snakes of America chose you for their stupid war?

I would choose to be incarcerated as Mohammed Ali had done before.

What if those political morons never took prayer out of this country's schools?

The graduation rate would fly through the roof and God would be honored, too.

What if you had to carry the weight of the world, would it be too hard for you to lift?

If you were strong enough to carry that weight, you would never have to ask, "what if".

"Overnight"

In life, anything worth having is usually acquired by some form of a fight.

There are so many unseen rules to life's game, and they cannot be learned overnight.

We really don't need all of life's material riches nor the stress it sends us through.

I have learned that true riches are not measured in dollars, but by your family standing beside you.

So many of us can be hardheaded and I know one that fits perfectly in this class.

It's funny how quickly everything can go bad, as you pray that this burden will soon pass.

Take your time my friend and learn to slow down, there is no need to be in a rush.

And living life on the other side of the law keeps you stressed and wondering who you can trust.

Always show love to those who have shown that they have love for you.

But continue to try and love everyone because that's what Christ has shown us to do.

You can reach any goal you set, just be sure that your intentions are right.

Whatever you want out of life, you can have, but don't expect it overnight.

"Help!"

There are times when we are so self-consumed, and can only think of the problems that pertain to ourselves, be merciful be it friend or foe that has cried out to you for help.

Help is a word that can take so many distinct forms and cover every base.

Because help should be given unconditionally it plays no favorites toward gender or even race.

Don't wait to only hear one's call for help, for there are far too many too proud to ever ask.

You don't have to be rich to help someone; many times the help needed doesn't require cash.

Just think about all the times you asked for help and were hurt by the reality of being ignored.

As for myself, I have chosen to help my brothers and sisters, I was taught this by Christ my Lord.

The greatest joy that is received is from helping the children; they hold the keys to our future. They must be taught how to love and to teach one another that compassion cannot be found on a computer.

All that is asked of you is to look at yourself and see over time how much unearned love and help you have felt. Once you see the sparkle in the eye of another, then you will understand the importance of rendering help.

"Strength"

The ability of the gifted to stand when others fall is truly heaven sent. And if you are one of God's many chosen, this gift you've been given is called strength. Many times, in our lives, it would be so easy to fold or to give up on living. But through the mind of my son, inner strength was mine from the very beginning. Some sit blind to the fact that any adversity conquered without death only increases your strength.

In simple terms, whatever trial you go through and continue to breathe was well worth the time spent. Through the eyes of a child, many of us can be viewed as a superman.

During their youth don't crush their vision, but take the time to help them to understand. I have contemplated removing myself from this world of pain and give back my destructive life. I continue to fight that demon of death, because I know this is right in my Father's sight. Today, my life is under construction to repair my spiritual car from my many collisions that left my life bent.

I now walk alone through life, but it is okay, because to see my son's little face gives his daddy strength.

Dedicated to Derson

"Lessons"

We all must be taught at our own pace, and some of the harder ones serve as a blessing.

There may be tears by night, but joy tomorrow, as life teaches each of us its lessons.

Many of us are slow to listen, but we are so quick to try and speak.

While others are slow to learn, but they want the reigns to try and teach.

We all have a role in life that must be found, and we are wasting precious time guessing.

There must be a time made for peace and solitude to be taught a lesson.

Those who are hardheaded and stubborn may be forced to master one lesson twice.

It is according to the severity of that lesson if the second time will or will not suffice.

You must know where you came from, for this will influence where your life is now headed.

Live life on life's terms, but shoot for the stars in your youth, or in your golden years you'll regret it.

I have spoken to you from my heart and my experiences to you are only my suggestions.

We must all stand ready and prepared for life's tutelage through its many ordeals and lessons.

"Still Waiting"

I have lost all faith in this wicked world where I am forced to dwell.

There in only pain and sorrow in this frigid and God forsaken prison cell.

This place is like a horror movie and I have given it an "R" rating.

As I try not to be consumed with hate and yet I am still waiting;

I was told as a youth that too much "weight" would break the bridge. This long process that takes my breath is how I'm now forced to live.

My mind and body have grown weak and now I must give them both rests.

The last years of my life have been wasted trying to pass the wrong test.

I feel so alone even if I am in a room full of unwanted company;

The pain in my heart pours out of my mouth, and the weak ones run from me.

This world of doom should be avoided at all cost.

Once you are trapped in agony's web, the hungry spider will assure you lost.

I take special medication to ensure my sanity and that is not up for debating.

My Lord holds the key that will set me free, as I am still patiently waiting.

"The Truth"

When one has been repeatedly lied to, your word is nothing and there must be proof.

If we would only keep it real with ourselves and man up and just tell the truth.

Some may ask what we consider as the truth in these last sinful days.

This world in which we live was founded on lies and now it seems that only crime pays.

Our children live day to day in a society that awaits their utter destruction.

Kids these days never earn what they get and therefore they are labeled as good for nothing.

This country is falling apart, and our leaders' choices cannot be respected.

Ever since this clown has been in office, just living in America has been so very hectic.

Soldiers wonder why they can't come home and literally hate that they are U.S. troops.

They risk their lives daily for a country that has never told them the whole truth.

We must find the answers we seek because this country is slowly running out of time.

America is in a war that is not ours and Bin Laden can't be this hard to find.

No matter my stature in society, I am still just a nigga they want in a noose.

So, I will always get down how I live, and be man enough to handle the truth.

"Fishing"

When we are trying to find ourselves and start to realize what we're missing,

We must remain calm and practice patience, just like when you are fishing.

If you make any sudden moves or speak too loudly, you might lose your catch,

Just as in the lake of life if you aren't satisfied with what you caught you can always throw it back.

There must be time taken to figure out what will be your best bait.

If you have caught that special fish, or that special someone don't let your catch escape.

As you have learned by now, fish or people can be elusive and so strong willed.

It may be a long fight to crown the champ and to seal that emotional deal.

We must teach our kids the relaxation and the thrill of trying to catch a fish,

Just enjoying a beautiful day at the lake with dad is a time they won't soon forget. When you hook that big fish and reel him in as the water across the lake is glistening, you are teaching your child some of life's many lessons, simply taking them fishing.

"Out of Time"

We must be thankful because every day is a blessing just to see the sunshine.

Some days I don't appreciate the simple things and feel I have emotionally run out of time.

There is no feeling worse than to feel all alone and that your loved ones don't really care.

The only feeling that could be worse is to suffocate and have your lungs run out of air.

Life is so short, so be sure to maximize your time down to the very last minute.

This world must continue to turn if you are or if you are not in it.

Always try to use this time that you have been given to constantly spread joy and love,

Our Heavenly Father placed us here for that very purpose which came divinely from above.

Many have fallen victim to that mental clock slowing down its ticks and its tocks.

You may become frustrated when it slows down just imagine your feelings when it stops.

A lot of the time I have been given I like to use for my poetry and rhyme.

I hope that future generations will still enjoy my work when I have finally run out of time.

"A New Day"

Every day that is made, upon completion is pushed off the cliff of endless days into the sea of yesterday, and like a flower that blossom in the Spring, a new day is molded, formed, and ultimately created. No one day is created identical to neither the next nor the prior day. A new day is a spell-binding occurrence, a sheer phenomenon that is so breathtaking that at some point and at some time, we all have stood stunned by the dawning of a new day. This new day that I speak of is by no means the greatest of the Creator's creations, but it is an affair that lovers have cherished for many a season. To stand arm-in-arm, hand-in-hand… with that one living soul whom you simply adore, as the death of one era gives birth to a new, is simply a gift from heaven and must be treasured for its magnificent splendor which is beyond compare. Do you agree that the very essence of a new day is glorious? If you don't agree, just imagine that today is the last new day that you were fortunate to behold. Now, I'm sure that you see that we can never underestimate the power of a new day.

"Time for A Change"

All of the sorrow that lay before you was placed there before your birth. Our Heavenly Father already knew all the answers and how long you would endure the hurt. There are so many who have stumbled, and they have chosen to wallow in their pain,

It's essential that we understand, we must stand up again, and realize, it's time for a change. Many of us despise our situations, but we see that a change must be made.

That change is sometimes unavoidable for our true foundation to be laid. We often get stuck in a routine that has forced us into a spiritual rut.

When you lack self-control and discipline, it becomes almost impossible to pick yourself up.

Living a fruitful life can be a self-fulfilling and a joyous episode,

But if your life is not perfect, we can find ourselves crushed under its heavy load.

You might stay totally focused on your needs and wants and keep your prize in close range, stay mentally sharp enough to realize when there comes a time for a change.

"Cherish the Day"

The beginning of our lives was a special and calculated moment for our parents, or was it a night of hot, lust-filled passion. No matter the case, we were conceived and brought into this world. We went from a twinkle in our father's eye to a bouncing baby in our father's lap. Our mother nurtures us with tender love and spoiled us to our core. The transformation from being that toddler trying to walk, to running care-free through the school yard with the other children is so amazing. This time in our lives is without a doubt the most important, as we learn the basics of developing from a child into a young adult. This time is also overlooked by the child as a special time in their lives. Before you know it, you are a teenager, and in such a hurry to become an adult, not realizing that life's stages are increasingly severe as you passes into adulthood. Now, you are the grown up that you always dreamed of being. You must do for yourself now, and according to the choices that you made in your past, your immediate future is not all candy and ice cream as you may have previously thought it to be. I stand today as one of the many that would love to turn back the hands of time and have a chance to do some things differently, and enjoy my childhood to the fullest, but of course we all know that it is an impossibility. I beg of you, parents, to allow your children to be children, and explain to that there is no need to rush to grow up.

Help them to understand that the best years of their lives are the ones that they are experiencing right now. For you, it seems as though time is standing still for them and they have no cares in this world. Help them to cherish the day.

"Keep It Moving"

This life that we lead can sometimes feel like an optical illusion,

But it generally tends to feel that way when we need to keep it moving. It is a fact of life that we all will come to see and must overcome,

And we cannot get caught up in our feelings and back down or run. You are the captain of the ship and the Lord is the deep blue sea.

There must be a general respect for who provides you help and that is the key.

If you never find a way to tap into your inner thoughts, feelings, and fears,

Your next step could be fatal, and you can't always trust in your peers.

There is a factor of respect that must be shown and then it will be given,

A lot of us tend to complain like children, and whine about the way we are living.

We must keep our minds focused on reaching our goals instead of worrying about losing.

You need not get stuck on stupid and realize that we must keep moving.

"Shame"

It's so hard to survive in this cruel world so it tries to drive me insane.

With children dying and mothers crying the way we live is a crying shame.

My life is so hard to make better, when it's obvious that this life I lead is not fair.

While living in the skin where in life becomes a game of truth or dare.

I can't afford to tell the truth, but this world has dared me to lie.

This catch-22 that I'm stuck in leaves me asking myself, "why?"

I am trapped in this skin I am in and it's the color of darkness or black rain,

But unlike me, those fortunate to be the color of clouds seem to have mastered this game.

Our children are the last hope we have, so we must show them a better way.

We must turn off the T.V. and help them to see that selling drugs and shooting guns is not okay. It's a crying shame the way that our women cry out for the strength of her black man,

And her reality is that they are all homosexual or stuck in Federal prison.

Our confused black youth are stuck in a cycle that we must help them to change.

So, until we stop living for today and start praying for tomorrow, this life is a damn shame.

"Need"

Some settle for just a small portion while others take all they can out of greed.

I don't want more than my fair share because that is all that I will need.

When the Lord was handing out what we need many of us thought he said greed.

This mistake was made by the selfish and their ways will not allow them to succeed.

Small problems tend to grow and spread throughout our lives like a deadly virus.

For example, many non-smokers will die from second-hand smoke, while the smoker lives on right beside us.

I am using simple dialect to try and reach the many complex minds of this day.

There are too many so-called chiefs and not enough eager Indians any damn way.

So, you must get down how you live, and if you don't work you don't eat.

If we don't strive to change our futures, then our past we are doomed to repeat.

I simply want to live my life and make things comfortable for my wife and my seeds.

We tend to make our lives hard on ourselves when our demands exceed our needs.

"Alone"

There are so many of us that function best by ourselves away in our own little zone.

This is not as complicated as one may believe because some operate better alone.

Socializing with others is not always as easy as one individual may think.

When you seem to be unable to fit in groups you may feel like the weakest link.

The group sessions are not always best for a person who likes their own space.

The ability to recognize you work best alone has nothing to do with color or race.

Some seem to work well with a team, but for others, it just complicates things.

So, it is okay for you to be more comfortable alone and the least amount of stress that it brings.

Throughout history, there have been several scholars who accomplished solo goals.

There was Lance Armstrong and Jesse Owens and there are countless others who fill these roles.

If you like being by yourself, it is okay and don't allow anyone to say that you are wrong. You just need your own individualized space and that comes along with you being more comfortable alone.

"Get Away"

We must put our lives in perspective and learn how to master our role today.

There will come a time in your life that calls for you to rest and get away.

The world will continue to turn by any means, and this will go unchanged,

Sometimes we are forced to live and learn and some of life's lessons will require some pain.

If we can just find that place in our minds in which we capture tranquility.

When that place in your mind is found, it will increase your growth and maturity.

The purpose of a getaway is to reward yourself with an overdue mental break.

And that break can also be physical, there is only so much that the body can take.

It becomes necessary for everyone to know when their body needs rest.

Some of us are more fortunate than others just continuing to breathe we're surely blessed.

There may be those that don't understand and for them what more can I say?

I want to walk on soft sand, a carefree man, on my much needed get away.

"Lost Your Focus"

During these trying times in our lives our loved ones may feel as though they don't know us.

If you have experienced this from your family then you have surely lost your focus.

The true mark of an individual's genius is measured in evolvement by which a score is given.

It may take several years for the goal to be reached so just continue to keep on living.

We can never lose sight of our goals as we conquer one, move swiftly to the next.

Never allow yourself to rest at a comfort level, a state of discomfort brings out our best.

This voyage that I speak of it will either destroy you or increase your strength,

Take full advantage of the advice that I give for which this lesson was meant.

When you take your eyes off your prize for a split second you have lost.

You must be prepared to fight for your life, truths, and beliefs at all cost.

There is a constant struggle for power which has been formulated to try to control us.

We may be blessed to foresee a developing disaster if we have not lost your focus.

"Reach!"

There are some of us put here to teach, and there are others to preach.

You may never know what you are capable of unless you learn how to reach.

In your mind you must not doubt your abilities, or accept the word "no",

If you don't believe in yourself when you are put under pressures, it will show.

There is a gigantic world out there, and you must act as though it needs you in it.

So, you must refuse to be told "you can't", "give up", or even "I quit".

The only one who can stop you is you, so never take your foot off the gas.

Always remember that haters will always hate you just switch lanes and continue to mash.

You must never be afraid to chase your dreams, no matter how long it may take.

When you are in the position that they said you couldn't get to, that's the icing on the cake.

We must continue to climb life's mountain no matter how high the peak. You must never give up on yourself and always continue to reach.

"Keep It Real"

Many black men try to prove how hard they are by the trigger of that blue steel.

There have been so many black males gunned down for so-called keeping it real.

We need to look to our future before we are forced to relive our past.

There is no justice for the ones whose missions include black gloves and a ski mask.

We see many black males who have lost their manhood, their heart and even their life.

Trying to jack one of our own kind who sat too long at the red light.

Drugs rule the country, and the U.S. government supplies us the most;

We don't own a plane or a boat to take drugs from coast to coast.

There are so many of our youth who have bled and died for their set.

They are just misguided and without a father figure trying to become an old school vet.

I will not apologize for the way I wrote this; it shows exactly how I feel.

There are too many brothers dead or in jail for trying to keep it real.

"A New Beginning"

Many of God's children have found themselves lost in our own realm of what reality and fantasy really means. The path that is less taken in many ways is the path that the masses should tread. In the process there must be an even greater understanding that to walk with the Father you must have an intimate relationship which will call for a new beginning. This new beginning that I speak of is the same as all choices we make, they are strictly free will.

The enemy will attempt by all means to meet you at the fork in the road to try and persuade you to take the "low road." An enchanted walk with the almighty is a special journey with the one and only higher power that loves every creation made from his precious hands. As life continues to evolve before your eyes, always remember that change is not always good to you but is at times so good for you. In every moment you are given air to breathe, if you need to make a positive change in life, never be afraid to embark on a new beginning.

"Complicated"

Change is not always best but in certain instances you should take it.

The occasional anger that comes with change can make our lives so complicated.

Living our lives day by day there are no two days that are the same.

We can be stuck in confusion and still not have the balls to make a change.

Your life was given to you alone and you are charged with making it your best.

Only you know what makes you happy or sad and you can't worry about the rest.

Our family and friends attempt to give us advice which may or may not be met. We must stand on our own two feet and give ourselves a reality check.

A lot of times we don't follow our first mind which has been sent from above.

Your first mind never lies, and I put that on everything that I love.

Allowing too many people to help you make your decisions is so overrated.

Pray to God and have faith in yourself and life won't be so complicated.

"Time"

There seems never to be an adequate amount of it in every day that goes past.

When we speak about time, it comes and goes entirely too fast.

I have gained a new respect for time since it is now what I'm forced to do.

Sitting lifeless in this concrete hell feeling as though my life is through,

Some people spend too much time concerned about the next man's business.

Those people tend to waste valuable time and I have God as my witness.

Learn to use your time wisely because once it's gone, you can never get it back.

Keep your mind occupied with positive thoughts and stay sucka free to be exact.

Don't be foolish enough to believe that you can somehow learn to freeze time.

You must realize that quality time is precious and always keep that in the back of your mind.

You must always remember that the life we live is a relentless uphill climb.

Don't make your life into a rat race and always realize that you must cherish your time.

"Runnin"

Every day is a God-given gift, and we must appreciate the gift that we have been given. The activities that make up our day keep our minds runnin'. There is no simplicity to the task that is taken by the ones who comprehend the importance of the evolvement of the mind and its many stages. The world will continue to elevate itself with or without you. If you see life as your greatest opponent, then you are correct, and that ability to understand your adversary is essential. You must not run from, but toward this juggernaut called life. The tests of this life and the next must be mastered completely. The main element for you to keep runnin' is to become mentally strong. We as a people tend to over exercise our bodies, and under exercise our minds, knowing full well that the brain is the greatest muscle that we possess. The more we intensify our thought process, the more fueled we are to keep on runnin'. The correct use of the mind allows you the freedom to have no limitations. If one was to discontinue relying on the mind that automatically hinders mental growth, and mental growth is required to enhance the solitude of the mind that allows a human being to co-exist. So, with that said, we must catch our breath and keep on runnin'.

Section Five

MY SPIRITUAL JOURNEY

"Unbreakable"

This pain that I must bear has overflowed and is without doubt unmistakable,

But the strength of the mind and intervention divine has made my spirit unbreakable.

I must never lose sight of my blessings in a world that is oh so very cold,

As I continue to walk toward that light with eyes filled with tears, red, and half-way closed. If a man has never seen death face to face, he is nothing more than a shell.

Living this life keeps me under pressure, but a dead man tells no tales.

"Love" can "curse" you out just like any other four-letter word.

And "love can be a "curse" in these streets when you're caught making love to those birds. I have been on my knees and constantly asking my God why?

Why have thou forsaken me when I need you the most and I know you can hear my cries?

"We" knew this had to happen to me to be alive for my life's next lessons.

God said, "I am always here", but my only son has asked of me the same question.

Lord, please hear me, "this burden is too much to bear and my mind is no longer stable."

My child, you have stood where so many others have fallen and through me, our Lord is truly unbreakable.

"Faith"

We saints pray for forgiveness, peace, or whatever may be the case.

When we patiently wait on our Lord to move, this is what we call faith.

No matter the circumstances you must never doubt what you believe.

Just continue to pray, open your heart, and prepare yourself to receive.

There must always be a bridge, between you and your precious prayers.

Jesus came to cross that bridge and make the walk up Heaven's stairs.

If you don't believe in faith, what will it take to show you it exists?

Some of our most difficult trials of faith are the temptations we must resist.

Just because we can't see Him, does that mean that Christ is not there?

A lot of us have lost our faith due to our failure to prepare.

I will continue to wait on the Lord, as He continues to work on me.

Heavenly Father, no matter what I go through, I will always trust in Thee.

He promised never to give us more that we can handle on our life's plate.

Sometimes, it may seem He has left us, but He is just testing our faith.

Dedicated to My Heavenly Father

"Why Try?"

When you feel as though all hope is lost, just lift your head to the sky.

Our Father is waiting for us to ask for help when the enemy asks us, "why try?"

Honest and faithful effort is all that is asked, and all the rest will soon be added. A closed mouth will never get fed but remember to ask by faith and you shall have it. Sometimes the road will not be easy, but don't you every think of turning back.

That is when Satan attacks us the most, and we all must realize that.

We sometimes get frustrated and ask ourselves why have faith"
and why even bother? Jesus in flesh form mastered faith and
miraculously walked on water.

Never tell yourself that you can't make it, because you can if
you only try.

If you would only believe, our Father can teach you how to fly.

Always remember that you are special and please never stop
loving you.

If you can love yourself, then God's work in your life will
come shining through.

Continue to help those still in the dark to find His marvelous
light.

Don't worry about who will see your good deeds, nothing gets
past God's sight.

Keep your knees bent in prayer and your head and hands
stretched toward the sky.

We serve an awesome God, and His grace and mercy are the
reasons why we try.

"My Special Friend"

Many years have gone past and many so-called friends have
done the same.

The ones that claim to be your best friends tend to cause you
the most pain.

A true friend will pick you up each time that you fall.

That true friend will always answer the phone no matter how late you call.

My special friend is pure and will come running when I call His name.

This is the same friend that will rush right in and ease my pressures and pain.

If I need to speak to my friend, that call is toll free.

But if by chance I call collect, He always pays the fee.

It would be selfish on my part to ask Him to love only me.

He showed His love for each and all when He died on Calvary.

He's my only true friend and I have entrusted Him with my life.

My special friend wants to be yours, too, and His name is Jesus Christ.

"Perfect"

To be like a flawless diamond may not calm one's desire to be rich. We must realize to be considered as flawless, you are tagged as being perfect.

The ambitions of one rider can allow you to strive only for the best.

Allowing yourself to be held to such high standards can be an overwhelming quest.

There are many of us, who try to purchase perfection and realize that it cannot be bought,

But on our troubled road in search of perfection, many of life's lessons shall be taught.

Coming to the realization that our life is what we tend to make it,

Make your early decisions your best, or this cruel world will try to take it. We must all understand that there is power and strength in large numbers.

If we would just learn to believe in ourselves, we will see that we can do wonders. Perfection is a state of mind and only one person has lived up to that life.

That life that I speak of goes without saying, it belonged to Jesus Christ.

"Letter to My Ex-Employer - - Lucifer"

Dear Lucifer:

I am writing you this letter to finalize a few issues with you while I have some free time. My many faithful years to Death, Inc., I know has had me on your mind.

During those years I felt you were a benefit, which all the time you and your job were just a dead end.

You tried to rob me of my life, but you could only help pave my way to this Federal Pen.

Your use of lies and deception was masterful, but why wouldn't it be, at mass destruction you are the best.

Lying, killing, and stealing are your full-time job and the joy it brings you continues to fuel your evil quest.

I have come to realize why you work so many hours; you know your time here is so limited,

Yeah, I know you have built a huge company and thank God that I am no longer part of it.

Why do you tremble with fear" Is it from the sound of my new employer's name?

I almost forgot you once worked for Him, too, but your lust for power forced you into the game of pain.

There were so many lives of good people I destroyed, and this would have never happened without you.

This letter confirms my resignation from your firm and I am completely through with you and it. My new career is filled with promise, and my co-worker network is the best in the business. You will never again be rendered my services and for this reason, my letter had to be sent.

Thank you for nothing, DP

"Promise"

What is a promise? As I see it, nothing more than a verbal commitment.

As in any other commitment, once broken its severity can carry massive amounts of resentment.

I have broken so many promises, that I have long lost its count.

But understand as you break them the consequences for them will tend to mount.

In the eyes of a woman or a child, a broken promise is nothing more than a gigantic lie.

Unfortunately, I have broken promises to both, and no excuse is adequate for "why?"

You are giving me your assurance that what you say will shortly come to pass.

For so many their word is all they have left and it's more valuable than any amount of cash.

In a perfect world, a promise would be irrelevant; the truth would be life's meat and bread,

But this world is so far from perfect, so well with that, enough said.

Judas lied on Jesus and many shall lie on you and they too may seal the lie with a kiss. What was once this world's greatest lie has evolved into this world's most divine promise?

"No Surrender"

Deep in the trenches is where the war for peace is either lost or won.

Every battle is between the opposing forces and it does not require the use of a gun.

Confrontation can be beneficial in terms of there being a champion to be rendered.

It must be fully understood that warriors will not retreat and must never surrender.

The crusade that I speak of has gone on since the beginning of time and is not a myth.

You must stay prepared for war with full armor and your decisions must be made swift.

We must realize that there is an evil army and there is one that is righteous and true, and before you pass from this world to the next, one of these rivals you must choose. The forces of evil have a mighty captain, whose mission is to rob, steal and kill,

But the leader of the just and righteous has come to impose His awesome will.

I hope you now realize that this war is between Jesus Christ and His arch enemy Satan. Every knee shall bow, and every tongue shall confess, so don't waste precious time debating. In this raging battle, my all-powerful Savior shall stand alone as the unanimous victor.

We must keep our faith and continue to fight because there can be no surrender.

"Heaven's Door"

This life is filled with obstacles and it can beat us down and so much more.

But if we could only speak to our fortunate loved ones who have walked through Heaven's door.

I hope that the door to enter Heaven is not as heavy as the door to enter this life.

For me to be at Heaven's door, I have paid the ultimate price.

This world in which we dwell is full of problems, pressures, and pain,

To gain the world and lose your soul is by no means an even exchange.

So many strong young soldiers have run out of time on life's continuing clock.

We have lost three of our vocal warriors in Jam Master J, Biggie and Tupac.

I hope that one day every lost soul will finally rest in peace.

But for now, it remains hard as we lay deep in the belly of the beast.

The road that we are forced to travel will pound us down to our very core.

I have repented of my sins, so Lord, I want in; it's just me knocking on Heaven's door.

"Driven"

As damnation stands at my door, I get in the car with madness and away I am driven.

I am driven to the verge of my life is, or is not, worthy of me to go on, living.

Life to me once was so valuable, but my motivation to live is no longer a must.

My back is filled with bloody knives and my eyes now see how Christ must have felt about Judas.

If you love life, hold tight to it, for with any love must come a trial by fire.

You must never give in to life's mental exhaustion nor your flesh as it begins to tire.

To be driven you must drive so God directs you from the map of your life.

With you to drive and God to guide, and with His added help, your decisions are more precise.

When and if you make the mistake of making your own choices, suggestions, or verdicts, you will realize that your knowledge and comprehension of good and bad choices continue to be in conflict.

We all shall possess the opportunity to repent and ask the Fat her to be forgiven.

This option shall always be by free will, so do so and allow your life to be divinely driven.

"Sometimes Angels"

There are many stricken by poverty and their deprivation comes from so many reluctant angles. Those of us that show compassion in another's time of suffering may sometimes be helping angels.

The phrase "sometimes angels" reflects the opening of the heart as well as the mind.

As you are blessed by giving that derelict a dollar, it's not your concern if that dollar buys cheap wine.

If you were in the presence of an "angel" are you sure that you would even know?

Just because the cover of the book is filthy, you must read its contents to be for sho'.

An angel is a child or two of God's most beautiful and precious of His creations,

And for His children to reach out to help one another always gives the Father the utmost of jubilation.

Each and every one of us shall be in need of the help of one that is more fortunate.

As we also learn to pay attention to our brother's pain and this view is truly divinely sent.

In these last days, many have hardened their hearts and its Christ's job, not ours, to change those. But we must continue to be open-handed, for the many souls we help may sometimes be angel.

"Lost"

If there is no one looking for you, then how can you ever be found?

Our Savior searches for His sheep that have gone astray and His voice is the sweetest sound.

You must never harden your heart and always allow God to be your only boss.

When you feel alone and you don't know why, we must realize that we are lost.

Imagine, if you would, a world free from death, anger, and pain.

We must put our hand in the hand of that man or that pain can never change.

The enemy wants to kidnap our joy and have our happiness gagged and bound, but never forget that every sinner is a saint who just happened to fall down. Sometimes in my mind, I am a child searching for that magic place to walk on streets made of gold and finally see my Savior's face.

Happiness for you and me is priceless since Jesus already paid the cost.

Allow Him to be the head of your life and He will never again let you get lost.

"The Church"

We all have that special place that we share a comfort level with or without a group of individuals that is beyond compare. This place for me, and several others, is the church. The church is a rock that stands strong against all that oppose it. This rock will not be moved like the many grains of said of an oasis.

The church is a mighty tree that is deep rooted right beside a mighty free-flowing river. That tree will receive a continuous feeding from that mighty river, which will make the roots mighty also.

This is the same as our Heavenly Father increases our strength as we are blessed to come to His house. This mighty tree is also blessed with many branches that reach high towards the heavens. Those many branches represent the congregation of the church.

The church is my mighty rock and my mighty tree. I am one of the branches that are a part of the church. Our Heavenly Father provides nourishment for His people in the same way He provides the river for the mighty tree.

The church is my Father's house, and I will continue to give Him the praise and worship that He deserves. The church is holy, and the ground on which it stands is holy and the faithful congregation will raise their voices on high, as the Lord of Lords pours down His mighty and faithful grace upon them.

The church will always be a place of worship and the magnifying of our Lord. We, as saints, shall always need our church, and our church will always need its saints. If you have never visited or felt as though you were not worthy to attend a church service, you are so sadly mistaken. My God is waiting for you and will always be waiting for you in His house . . . the church.

"Stay Strong"

When the storms of life are raging, and you don't know why everything is going wrong.

This is the time in your life that you give it to God and continue to stay strong.

It may seem as if you are all alone, and you are constantly under the enemy's attack.

In those trying times in our lives, we must rest in God's bosom as He carries us on His back.

I have been through my own personal hell, but I kept my faith none the less.

We can't always walk through our trials; we may have to crawl through to be blessed.

The times you feel you are at your lowest, are the times you must praise God the most.

And when He brings you through, continue to stay humble, for only fool's brag and boast.

He never said that the road would be easy, but through Him, ye shall overcome.

In order to be found worthy of our blessings, we can't always walk, we may be called to run.

Never put your faith in a mere man, there has been only one divine, and now He is gone.

He is now in heaven preparing for His glorious return, but until that day, we must stay strong.

"Lying Still"

I should have chosen the well-lit path, as I reach into the dark agony is all I'm allowed to feel.

I've learned a priceless lesson from this laceration called incarceration, as I am patiently lying still.

So many years have escaped me, and they shall now fly free forever. The desire for freedom is my only ambition that has merged these words.

Growing through the pain I've tried 2 abandon that belief of an eye for an eye, and I reserve the right 2 kill.

But if you take one of mine, I'll take 10 of yours so I suppose I've just been lying still.

I am ashamed that I yet possess this obsession for my hustle, which has destroyed my bloody past.

As momma taught me 2 pray to Christ, my block taught me 2 to grind and pray for straight cash.

Please allow me to hope for better days, as tears in my son's eyes have completely broken my will.

My will 2 do it all again and do life in the pin, where so many black men are patiently lying still.

About the Author

Derrick Pratt is a man that has risen above his circumstances and found his journey to freedom in both mind and body through his poetic expressions. Through his journey the three phases of this life were revealed to him and he will share them with you. LIFE IS HELL ON EARTH. The first phase is the introduction to HELL'S GATES. The second phase and most difficult is the bowels of Hell (THE BELLY OF THE BEAST). The last and final phase is THE RELEASE FROM HELL. It must be acknowledged that these three phases are repeated ENDLESSLY.

www.ingramcontent.com/pod-product-compliance
Lightning Source LLC
Chambersburg PA
CBHW051839040426
42447CB00006B/607